ISBN 978-1-943159-24-6

The publisher would appreciate notification where errors occur so that they may be corrected in subsequent printing and/or editions. Please send comments to the publisher by emailing to deeprivers67@yahoo.com

Printed in the United States of America

Chronic Faith

A believer's approach to chronic illness and pain

WORKBOOK

How to Use This Workbook

This workbook was designed to be used in conjunction with the book, *Chronic Faith,* as a way to help readers apply the concepts found within the book to their everyday lives. It can be used individually or in a group setting.

For individual use:

- Prior to beginning each chapter, please read the corresponding chapter in the book.
- Be sure to pray for wisdom and understanding before you begin.
- If you discover that certain topics are difficult to work through on your own, consider contacting a trusted minister, pastor, mentor, or counselor. Pray for the leading of the Holy Spirit before sharing your discoveries.
- Use the "Notes" pages to write down any revelations or reflections you wish to revisit at a later time. As you read Scripture passages referenced in the book or workbook, write down what they mean to you. Also, use this section to write down questions you want to research, pray about, or discuss with a trusted minister, pastor, mentor, or counselor.

For use with groups:

- It is recommended that answering questions remain optional for the emotional safety and health of all participants.
- While participants should be encouraged to complete the pages prior to the meeting, they should not be forced to share their responses. Grace should be extended to those who have not completed the pages.
- The facilitator might choose to generalize certain questions, asking "What activities might someone enjoy…?" or "What are some things a person in this situation could do?" so that no participant feels pressured to be transparent beyond their level of comfort.
- If participants choose to share personal reflections, that is entirely permissible and they should be received without judgement.
- Facilitators should be careful to create a safe space for all participants, reminding them that thoughts shared by others in each meeting should not be discussed outside the meeting.

Contents

Hello, my friend!

Thank you for choosing to embark on this **Chronic Faith** journey. As you complete the pages in this workbook, I pray that you would take full advantage of the opportunity to really examine your mindset and the way you perceive your diagnosis. The most effective way to engage with this material is to be as open as possible when reflecting on the questions, Scripture passages, prayers, etc. that you will find in these pages.

It is my prayer that the things you discover about yourself and your relationship with God will help you to see yourself even more clearly as God sees you. May you always focus more on your abilities than your limitations, maximize your quality of life, and pursue the purpose God has ordained for you. Blessings!

Expect Great Things,

Alli

CHAPTER ONE: The Journey

1. What was your initial reaction (emotional) to your diagnosis?

2. What, if anything, helped you to process this new information?

3. Who was the first person you told?

4. How did they react?

5. What do you say to yourself when you have a difficult day?

6. Write about a time when you forced your body to perform and it backfired.

____

7. What are some major events you have had to miss due to your diagnosis?

____

____

____

What emotions did you experience at the time?

____

____

____

Looking back, how do you feel about your decision?

____

____

____

____

8. When have you had to trust a loved one to do something you are used to doing for yourself?

____

____

____

____

9. List ten things in your life that you consider to be "Blessings" so that when you need to, you can refer to them?

_______________________________   _______________________________

_______________________________   _______________________________

_______________________________   _______________________________

_______________________________   _______________________________

_______________________________   _______________________________

10. The five stages of grief are ______________________, ____________________,

______________________, ____________________, ____________________.

Have you been through all of the phases? ☐ Yes ☐ No

How did your faith inform each stage? _________________________________

____

____

____

____

____

11. What are some more positive ways to re-state the following?
I am in so much pain. ____

____

I can't do things the way I used to. ___________________________________

____

I don't feel like doing anything—I'm so lazy. __________________________

____

Nobody understands what I'm going through. ____________________________

____

12. What Scripture will you allow to be a reminder of what God says about
you? ____

____

____

____

____

13. What is the true significance of "acceptance" as it relates to a diagnosis?

____

____

____

____

NOTES

CHAPTER TWO: Acceptance

1. What steps have you taken to educate yourself about your diagnosis?

   ____

   ____

   ____

   ____

2. What questions do you still have about your diagnosis? _______________

   ____

   ____

   ____

3. Take a moment to look up those answers. Make a note of them and where
   you found the information. ______________________________________

   ____

   ____

   ____

   ____

4. What are some symptoms or factors with which you identify most? ______

   ____

   ____

   ____

5. Are there chores or routine tasks that have become more difficult to
   complete since your symptoms began? List them. ___________________

   ____

   ____

   ____

6. How can you break them down into phases? Are there
   items/gadgets/devices you can use to assist you in completing the tasks?

   ____

   ____

7. Approximately how many hours of sleep do you get per night? ____________

8. Do you wake up feeling rested? Yes [ ] No [ ]

9. Do you take naps? Yes [ ] No [ ]

10. What is a restful activity that tends to refresh you? _____________________

_____

11. What parts of getting ready for the day do you find most challenging?
    (check all that apply)

[ ] waking up fully [ ] getting out of bed [ ] taking the first steps of the day
[ ] showering [ ] washing your hair [ ] brushing your teeth [ ] drying off
[ ] shaving [ ] moisturizing [ ] styling your hair [ ] preparing clothes
[ ] putting on make-up [ ] getting dressed [ ] putting on socks and shoes
[ ] other(s) ____

12. Take a moment to think about what makes those tasks difficult. What are
    some adjustments you can apply that might make them easier? __________

13. Do you feel self-conscious when using assistive devices? Yes [ ] No [}

14. Why or why not? ____

15. Are these feelings/ concerns more important than your well-being? Yes [ ]
    No [ ]

16. If your pride is keeping you from using devices that will improve your quality of life, but you're ready to prioritize your well-being over your pride, consider praying this prayer:

> *Dear Jesus,*
>
> *Thank You for Your grace and for taking care of me each and every day. Even through the pain and sickness, You have been faithful to provide everything I have needed. Today, I ask that You would please forgive me for allowing my pride to make decisions for me where my health and safety were concerned. I am sorry that I refused the things that You allowed to be made for my benefit. Please help me to embrace the things that will make my life better so that I can conserve my energy for important things like living out my God-given purpose. Thank You for hearing me when I pray. In Jesus' name.*
>
> *Amen.*

17. What are some tools/resources that might be beneficial to you and how might you access them? ____

____

____

____

____

____

<table>
<tr><td>

Consider this:

Before spending a lot of money out of pocket for assistive devices, check with your doctor. Many of these items can be prescribed by a physician and medical insurance may cover some or all of the cost.

</td><td>

"I have a very simple philosophy. One has to separate the abilities from the disabilities. The fact I cannot walk, that I need crutches or a scooter or whatever it is, has nothing to do with my playing the violin."

–Itzhak Perlman, violinist

</td></tr>
</table>

NOTES

CHAPTER THREE: From Sickness to Witness

1. How do you behave when you are sick? _________________________
____
____
____

2. Now, ask 3 people how they think you behave when you do not feel well?
____
____
____
____
____
____

3. What are some healthy ways to approach moments when you just want to check out? ____
____
____
____

4. Try keeping a journal for seven days. What patterns do you see emerging?
____
____
____
____

5. Are there people in your life to whom you owe a "thank you"? Make a list here and think about ways you would like to show your appreciation.

Person I Want to Thank   *How I Want to Thank Them*

____
____
____
____
____

6. Make a Gratitude List. Write down ten things for which you are grateful. Commit to reading this list 2-3 times per week.

My Gratitude List

I am grateful for:

1) ____
2) ____
3) ____
4) ____
5) ____
6) ____
7) ____
8) ____
9) ____
10) ____

7. Are there people in your life who do not understand your diagnosis or its effects? List these people below and next to their names, write something that you wish they could understand. If the opportunity to address these concerns presents itself, you will have a place to start the conversation.

Name   **What I wish they understood**

____
____
____
____
____
____

____

Attitude of Gratitude

Living with chronic illness brings with it a lot of challenges, but the challenges are not who you are and they do not have to change your disposition or your personality. Walking in gratitude is part of God's will for our lives because keeping our blessings in mind helps us balance the more difficult parts of our lives so that we do not focus solely on them. According to research published by Harvard Medical School, "Gratitude helps people feel more positive emotions, relish good experiences, improve their health, deal with adversity, and build strong relationships." (https://www.health.harvard.edu/healthbeat/giving-thanks-can-make-you-happier). As you make the decision about what kind of patient, friend, relative, and person you want to be, keep this verse in mind.

"Give thanks in all circumstances; for this is God's will for you in Christ Jesus."
—1 Thessalonians 5:18 (NIV)

NOTES

CHAPTER FOUR: Where is God?

Take a moment to become aware of God's presence with you. In this moment, without asking for anything, just express to Him how you feel. Envision all of your cares ascending to Him.

1. Make a list of times when God has heard and answered your prayers.

____

____

____

____

____

____

Lord, thank you for being a prayer-answering God. I know you have made ways before. You have been a faithful Protector, Provider, Savior, Redeemer, Comforter, and Fried. Please help me to place my full confidence in you again because you do not change. In Jesus' name. Amen.

2. List several things you are asking God to do. As you pray, ask God to align your prayers with His will for your life, then believe that He will respond.

____

____

____

____

____

NOTES

CHAPTER FIVE: Misinterpretations of Faith

1. Recall a time when you or someone you know received a miracle.

   ____

   ____

   ____

   ____

Lord Jesus, you are the same Miracle Worker that turned water into wine, calmed a raging sea, healed the sick, and raised the dead. I believe that you are the same Jesus and I honor you. My hope in you will not be determined by what I see or feel, but by Who you are. No matter what, you are good and you are God. In Jesus' name, I pray. Amen.

Jesus Christ is the same yesterday and today and forever. –Hebrews 13:8

2. How has God blessed you since your diagnosis? How has He used others to be a blessing to you?

   ____

   ____

   ____

   ____

   ____

   ____

3. Are there miserable comforters in your life? _______________ Did/ do you believe them? _______________ Read Psalm 41.

4. What does the Lord do for the weak? _______________________________

   ____

   ____

5. What did the writer's enemies say about him? _______________________

   ____

   ____

6. What did his close friend do? ___________________________________
____

7. How does the writer know that God is pleased with him?

____

____

Read the following verse every day until you have it memorized:

The LORD sustains them on their sickbed and restores them from their bed of illness. –Psalm 41:3

8. Aside from your physical body, what other parts of your life have been negatively impacted by your diagnosis?

____

____

____

____

Lord, I know that you are a Healer and that seeing me sick does not make you happy. So, by faith, I am reaching out to you for your healing virtue. Please heal me and make me whole. In Jesus' name, I pray. Amen.

Healing is the children's bread,

And we're invited to God's table.

Despite physical limits,

It is God Who makes us able.

Our diagnoses mean

We have an opportunity

To look into the mirror

And to see what God might see.

God has a plan for every pain

In life that we have faced.

Although He does not cause it,

With Him, nothing goes to waste.

So, however difficult life is

Or how big your problems seem

Your life is marked with purpose—

There's nothing He can't redeem!

NOTES

CHAPTER SIX: Identity Theft

1. List five activities in which you can engage regularly in order to be a blessing to someone.

    a. ____

    b. ____

    c. ____

    d. ____

    e. ____

2. What are you good at?

    ____

    ____

    ____

    ____

    ____

3. What activities do you enjoy?

    ____

    ____

    ____

    ____

    ____

4. What are some unique things about you?

    ____

    ____

    ____

    ____

    ____

What personal goals do you have? ____

____

____

____

____

NOTES

CHAPTER SEVEN: Tough Love

1. Name one person you know or have observed who has gone through a difficult medical journey with grace. ______________________________
    - What do you think empowered them to maintain their positivity or accomplish something special during their time of illness?

    ____
    ____
    ____
    ____

2. No one else is reading this, so feel free to be as candid as possible. What are some areas in which you know you could take better care of yourself?

    ____
    ____
    ____
    ____

3. Name three people or groups that you can help or offer support to in some way. See if there is at least one that you can help on a regular basis. (This can be financial, but it could also be praying for someone, calling occasionally to check on them, writing letters, crafting, baking cookies for a special kid's little league team, etc.)
    - ____
    - ____
    - ____

4. Name one thing you do regularly or have done recently that you wish you had said "no" to. ____

    ____
    ____
    ____

    Think about why you said "yes" and note your reason honestly here.

    ____
    ____
    ____

____

Would you make the same decision now? Why or why not? __________

____

____

____

____

5. List two tasks that you put unnecessary pressure on yourself to do that could actually wait.

____

____

____

6. What have you been waiting to do until you "feel better" (A hobby? A business? Exercise? A healthy relationship?)

____

____

____

____

What steps can you take today to move toward those pursuits?

____

____

____

____

____

____

> "I can do all things through Christ which strengtheneth me."
>
> –Philippians 4:13, KJV

NOTES

CHAPTER EIGHT: The Cost of Living

Do you know your value to God? The passage below is excerpted from Isaiah 43:1-4 (NIV).

¹ But now, this is what the LORD says— he who created you, Jacob, he who formed you, Israel: "Do not fear, for I have redeemed you; I have summoned you by name; you are mine.

² When you pass through the waters, I will be with you; and when you pass through the rivers, they will not sweep over you. When you walk through the fire, you will not be burned; the flames will not set you ablaze.

³ For I am the LORD your God, the Holy One of Israel, your Savior; I give Egypt for your ransom, Cush and Seba in your stead.

⁴ Since you are precious and honored in my sight, and because I love you, I will give people in exchange for you, nations in exchange for your life.

1. List three areas in which you might be able to cut expenses to make room in your budget.

   - ____
   - ____
   - ____

2. Write three questions that you want to ask your doctor at your next appointment that may help address your expenses.

   - ____
     ____
   - ____
     ____
   - ____
     ____

> "Making your health care affordable is an investment in your own destiny, and a return on God's investment in you."
>
> *–Chronic Faith*

NOTES

CHAPTER NINE: What if I die?

1. What activities fill your heart with true joy (Not entertainment, not amusement, but true joy)? _______________________

____

____

____

(If you can identify the things that bring you joy, you can make it a priority to engage in them.)

2. What gives your life meaning? _______________________

____

____

____

3. What is a decision you made this week that you regret making or what is a difficult decision that you made because you did not want to have regrets?

____

____

____

____

4. Using the chart below, shade in the hours you usually spend sleeping on an average day. Write in any other daily routines (exercise, meals, work, therapy, family, etc.). Are there opportunities to maximize your time?

12am	1am	2am	3am	4am	5am	6am	7am
8am	9am	10am	11am	12pm	1pm	2pm	3pm
4pm	5pm	6pm	7pm	8pm	9pm	10pm	11pm

NOTES

CHAPTER TEN: The Mindset of a Champion

1. What elements of your daily routine are non-negotiable? What activities are you committed to completing on a daily basis? _______________________

   ____

   ____

   Weekly? ____

   ____

   ____

   Monthly? ____

   ____

   ____

   (Be realistic—if you aren't sure you will be able to manage an item consistently, feel free to place a question mark next to it. Be sure to allow yourself grace when your body does not cooperate with your plans and be flexible in case the unpredictable occurs.)

2. If you've been sitting on the sidelines, watching the game instead of suiting up and playing, take the time to evaluate yourself now. How has your condition changed since your diagnosis? What have you figured out about your body and symptoms? _______________________________________

   ____

   ____

   ____

3. What is the first step toward a maximized quality of life for you?

   ____

   ____

   What is the second step? ____

   ____

   ____

   What is the third step?____

   ____

   ____

4. How would you describe yourself to others? ________________________

____

5. Do you think others see you this way? If not, how do you think others see
   you? ____

____

____

6. What is your prayer for yourself? _____________________________

____

____

____

____

____

____

____

____

____

____

7. Record instances in which you have seen God at work during your medical
   journey. Have there been silver linings, blessings in disguise, or unexpected
   encounters that provided strength for your journey? Make note of them so
   that they will continue to provide strength for you in the future.

____

____

____

____

____

____

____

____

____

NOTES

CHAPTER ELEVEN: Chronic Faith

How do you define faith? _______________________________________
____

Look up three Bible verses about faith.' Write them out below in the translation of your choice. Then write how you will apply the verse to your life.

1. Verse: ____
____
____
____

Where it's found: ____
Personal application: ____
____
____
____

2. Verse: ____
____
____
____

Where it's found: ____
Personal application: ____
____
____
____

3. Verse: ____
____
____
____

Where it's found: ____
Personal application: ____
____
____
____

NOTES

Medical History At-a-Glance

Last Name:	M.I.:	First Name:

Social Security Number		Date of Birth	_ _ / _ _ / _ _ _ _

Doctor's Name	Office Address	Phone Number	Type of Doctor

Prescription Information			
Drug	Dosage	When do you take it?	Type of medicine

Pharmacy	Address:	Phone:
Allergies		

Preferred Hospital		Insurance Provider	
Are you an organ donor?	☐ yes ☐ no	Do you have a DNR?	☐ yes ☐ no

Recent surgery/ procedure/ exam/ hospital stay	Location	Dates	Comments

Emergency Contact:	Phone:	Relationship:

www.ingramcontent.com/pod-product-compliance
Lightning Source LLC
Chambersburg PA
CBHW080353030726
47598CB00009B/2734